Ransom Neutron Stars
How to Start Your Own Crazy Cult
by Stephen Rickard

Published by Ransom Publishing Ltd.
Unit 7, Brocklands Farm, West Meon, Hampshire GU32 1JN, UK
www.ransom.co.uk

ISBN   978 178591 448 5
First published in 2017

How to Start Your Own Crazy Cult

Stephen Rickard

Do you want to start your own crazy cult?

You can be the cult leader. It's a great idea!

Lots of people will like you.
Lots of people will admire you.

That will make you feel good.

You will need to act like a cult leader.
You will need power and strength.

People must think you have all the
answers to the secrets of the universe.

It is not easy to start your own cult.

Here are some tips.

Looks

You need to look right.

Tall and slim is best.

Bald is not a good look.

If you have a bald patch, keep your hair short. Or you will just look crazy.

Don't be too hairy and don't smell.

Don't have bad breath. (Suck mints if you need to.)

Keep your fingernails clean.

Look smart.

Don't look rich.
Cult leaders often end up very
rich, but they must not show it.

Don't look poor.
People will think you are
crazy.

Looking "not-very-rich" is
about right.

How to act

You need to act like a cult leader.

Stay calm. You are wise.

You know the secrets of the universe.

Do not get stressed if your train is late.

Do not shout at the TV.

Be polite.

Getting followers

All cult leaders need followers.
If you have no followers, you have
no crazy cult.

Lots of people are looking
for a person to follow.
They need a person to tell them
what to think.

Make sure that person is you.

At first it is hard to get followers.

But keep trying.

Get helpers to spread the word.

As more people start to follow you,

it will get easier.

Look for lonely people.

Look for people with problems.

But don't look for people with **big** problems: they will want you to solve them.

Tell people that if they follow you, they can solve their problems on their own.

If they can't solve them, they are not trying hard enough.

Rich followers are better than poor followers.

Poor people don't have any money.

The next level

As your crazy cult grows, you need to move to the next level.

This is good. It means you can get other people to do the work.

You just turn up now and again and say things.

Say things that sound important
but don't mean anything.

Like:

    "Love everybody."

    "Be nice to animals."

    "Trust in me."

    "Help your friend."

    "I have the answer."

Don't appear with small groups of people.

Only huge crowds.

TV

TV is important.

You must look good on TV.

Don't do interviews on TV.

You will not be in control.

Only do TV when you are in
control.

When you are very rich, you can buy your own TV channel.

This is important. It will help your crazy cult grow.

Then you can say anything – and some people will believe you.

The big rule

The big rule is:

Don't get found out.

You can do anything in your private life, but make sure you keep it private.

Getting found out is the worst thing that can happen.

The last challenge

The last challenge is to make your crazy cult carry on after you are dead.

Then you are in the top ten of all-time crazy cults.

Of course you may not care, because you will be dead.

So why not spend it while you have it?

Have you read?

Fly, May FLY!

by Kathryn White

The Care Home

by Alice Hemming

Ransom Neutron Stars

How to Start Your Own Crazy Cult

Word count **562**

Green Book Band

Phonics

Phonics 1	Not Pop, Not Rock Go to the Laptop Man Gus and the Tin of Ham		*Phonics 2*	Deep in the Dark Woods Night Combat Ben's Jerk Chicken Van
Phonics 3	GBH Steel Pan Traffic Jam Platform 7		*Phonics 4*	The Rock Show Gaps in the Brain New Kinds of Energy

Book bands

Pink	Curry! Free Runners My Toys		*Red*	Shopping with Zombies Into the Scanner Planting My Garden
Yellow	Fit for Love The Lottery Ticket In the Stars		*Blue*	Awesome ATAs Wolves The Giant Jigsaw
Green	Fly, May FLY! **How to Start Your Own Crazy Cult** The Care Home		*Orange*	Text Me The Last Soldier Best Friends